D1373843

FIRST AID
FOR ENABLERS

TEN TREATMENTS
FOR ENABLERS
AND THE ADDICTS
THEY LOVE

Dr. David Curry
Author of *Bounce* and *God Plays Golf*

Dedicated to

Jonathan Jay Farvour
January 12, 1975 - July 25, 2000

Contents

First Aid for Enablers:
Ten Treatments for Enablers and the Addicts They Love
by Dr. David Curry

Published by Rescue Mission
702 Pacific Avenue
Tacoma, WA 98402

Cover and Interior Design by Tracy Taylor
Photograph by Nathan Golden

For sales and booking information, contact david@davidcurry.org

ISBN 978-0-615-51228-0

Printed in the United States of America

Author's Note

My hope is that this book will be a starting point in your understanding of enabling, codependent relationships. There have been many people who have been helpful in providing feedback on this manuscript including: Kate Curry, Lynette Grubbs, Les Doyle, Tracy Taylor, and Sue Snyder Turner. Their assistance was immensely helpful in creating what I hope is a readable book.

For editorial reasons, I have chosen to use the pronoun she/he in alternate chapters when referring to addicts. My hope is that this will assist more people in personalizing the advice within the book.

Treating the Wound

Where there is an addict, there is always an enabler. An addict who seeks to maintain some semblance of normalcy in relationships and function in society cannot do so without someone enabling them. Often more than one enabler is necessary for the addict to keep it all together. Supporting someone in addiction literally takes a village.

If you have picked up this book, it's likely because you already know there is a problem. When you see the word "enabling" you get an instant pang of hurt, guilt, panic and shame, all at once and indistinguishable from one another. There is someone in your life that you love, a person very precious to you, that has a problem. You have someone specific in mind when you read this book. That someone is special to you and you are hurting for her. The problem is that the addict is slowly, or perhaps not so slowly, killing herself with an addiction. And that is killing you.

You have an emotional wound because you can see all that the addiction has taken and threatens to take. It's stolen the addict's joy, health, freedom, and all or many of her healthy relationships. You know her well and you can list all the great and wonderful traits and characteristics you love about her. Yet you also know that she has changed; that she isn't the person you knew. It is as though you don't even know her anymore. The addict has become unpredictable, volatile, or perhaps withdrawn and depressed. She is different on the drug, and it's changed everything.

It's not as though you've neglected to try to fix it. This book didn't appeal to you as a study for a college class, or as an examination of human behavior. No, you're desperate. You have done all that you know how to do, offered to help numerous times, put untold hours and resources into reaching out to assist the addict that you love, yet nothing has worked. This first-aid kit might be your wake-up call, if you'll let it be.

Somewhere along the line, perhaps your spouse or a friend mentioned it to you; it occurred to you that you weren't a bystander in this addiction anymore. No, you were a part of the whole process; you were close to the situation, perhaps a little too close. You began to wonder if what you were doing to help and assist the addict in getting well wasn't actually making the problem worse. At the very least, you began to realize that it was controlling your life and having adverse effects on your finances, health and well-being. Is it possible that you seem to be more affected than the addict? At times you've wondered this, as she has moved from disaster to disaster and you've been left to deal with the fallout and cleanup.

You want to know if you're an enabler, or if you already know that you are an enabler, how you can stop being one and still help your son, daughter, friend or spouse get free from the destructive habit.

There is no doubt in my mind that you have enabled and assisted the addict in her addiction. Anyone who has been this close to an addictive person has enabled to one degree or another, if only out of ignorance of the addiction and how an addictive person manipulates and orchestrates things to make their life work. In my own life, as I look back on all the different personal and professional relationships that I've had with people who were struggling with addiction, I know that I've done things that were clearly enabling behaviors. Yet I didn't see it at the time.

So the pressure is off - you're one of us. You are one of the millions and millions of people who love someone who is addicted, and has tried to help them, only to later see that it wasn't the right thing to do. Don't read this book with a feeling of judgment or a self-flagellating spirit. Instead see this as a guidebook on your path to awakening to how pervasive enabling has become in your life, and how to get free and healthy. And that is the purpose of this book: It's time for you to get healthy.

Through this book I'll share plenty of direct, tactical advice on how to set up some healthy boundaries with your loved one. These will likely seem harsh and dogmatic, but they're terribly necessary and you mustn't ignore them out of hand. Instead, give them some thought. The longer this addictive pattern has been going on in your life, the more critical it is that you reset the way the relationship has functioned, and the harder it will be for you to do it. *But it is possible, and you can do it*. If you heed the advice and reset the boundaries in your life, it won't take too long before you start getting some much-needed perspective and the physical strength you need to achieve a healthy balance.

However, you must refrain from thinking that this book will help you get your loved one clean of her addiction. In fact, thinking that *you* are responsible for the other person getting clean and sober is one of the telltale marks of an enabling personality. This book is about helping you have a more balanced and appropriate relationship with the addict, who in turn can see benefits in her life if she chooses to respond. But this book has no magic pixy dust or formulas that can force someone to respond in the positive. If you choose to become healthy and set appropriate boundaries within your relationship, it is possible the addict will simply find someone else to enable her in the addiction.

Part of being healthy is knowing what you can control and what you cannot. All you can do - and what you *must* do - is create a healthy emotional life for yourself. Whether those around you respond in healthy ways is up to them. It is out of your hands. But then it always has been. You are just now beginning to understand that this is the case.

In *First-Aid for Enablers*, you're going to learn that you need to stop providing material assistance to the person you love. This is going to be hard for you to imagine, but you'll learn that by providing money, shelter, cars, food and other kinds of assistance, you have been keeping her from feeling the full weight of her decisions.

You will also learn many of the ways we are tempted to enable, how to set better boundaries, and what to expect after you set those boundaries. We'll look at practical steps to stop the destructive enabling cycle. They include the following:

✚ Educate yourself about addiction.

✚ Communicate unconditional love.

✚ Refuse to give financial & resource support.

✚ Be truthful about the addict's behavior.

✚ Hold the addict accountable for broken promises.

✚ Follow through; don't threaten.

✚ Extend loving words of encouragement.

✚ Be ready with next steps & solutions.

✚ Look for teachable moments.

✚ Be patient and consistent.

Most importantly, this book has a framework for you to understand that *you* must become healthy, both emotionally and spiritually, if you are going to be any help to the one you love who is caught up in the battle for her life. None of this is easy, although it is simple in the sense that you *can* do this. You *can* make better decisions, learn your lessons and come through this a stronger person.

If you've tried it all and it is not working, now is the time to do the right thing. Even if the right thing is the toughest thing you've ever had to do. It's time to draw a line in the sand. It's time to stop enabling. ✚

Getting Burned
While Trying to Help

Being an addict has been easier because of your help. For the over 30 million addicts in the United States, there are millions more who are allowing, excusing, or supporting addicts in their chaotic destruction. Undoubtedly there are many who even *encourage* people in their addiction. This is particularly common in relation to alcohol addiction. In one circumstance, I recall a father insisting that his alcoholic son have a drink with him immediately after he had come back from a rehab center. His reasoning, "I want my son to be able to hold his liquor. He's got to learn to control it." But his son couldn't control it and that drink set off a full decade of wild alcoholic behavior, culminating with the son losing everything he owned and ending up on the street.

But I didn't write this book for those misguided and ignorant enablers who are actively encouraging addiction. This book is written for those who, with the best intentions and from pure motives, have found themselves supporting and assisting someone they love, only to slowly realize that their well-intentioned assistance has created a secondary problem. They are now part of the addict's support system.

It is rare to come across a parent, sibling, or spouse who purposely tries to destroy someone they love by assisting the addict in addiction. However, it's quite common that people do it unwittingly, either because they don't understand addiction; they underestimate the power of addiction, or just can't accept that the person they love would do such a thing.

My presumption is that you're acting in love. You, as the reader, must be willing to come to another understanding: What you've done to help, up to this point, is actually hurting. The question you need to answer for yourself is this: *To what extent am I enabling the addict I love?*

The word enabling is often used, but rarely defined. It can be difficult for people to recognize it when it involves their own behavior. A simple definition is this:

Enabling is any behavior that removes or softens the consequences of addiction, thereby making it easier for the addict to continue to use drugs.

That means that *any* action you take that assists the addict could well be enabling destructive behavior. Even if that action was done with the best of intentions. Any action? Could that be right? One of the hardest things you have to confront is that even small assistance given to an addict, assistance that eases the stress created by their lifestyle, is enabling. Yet this awareness is fundamentally important to you becoming a positive influence in the addict's life, instead of being complicit in his demise.

Often I speak with grandparents who cannot resist the request of a grandchild for money, even if that grandchild is using it for drugs. Sometimes it is mother who goes behind the father's back to give support to a child who is using. She may threaten to leave the father if the child is kicked out, thus allowing the drug user to have a home base to manage a drug lifestyle. Each of these situations seems totally rational to the mother or grandparent who "feels" like it is the right thing to do. In fact, however, *any* activity that aids the drug user or cushions the consequence of his behavior will *prolong the addiction*. If you do these things, you are actually contributing to the problem.

There is a multitude of ways, some quite common, that people enable their loved one who is enslaved to drugs. Take this simple quiz to see if you are enabling or are tempted to enable.

1. Have you ever "called in sick" for the addict because he was too hung-over to go to work or school?

   ☐ Yes   ☐ No

2. Do you ever make excuses for the addict's drinking or behavior?

   ☐ Yes   ☐ No

3. Have you ever lied to *anyone* to cover up for the addict?

   ☐ Yes   ☐ No

4. Have you bailed the addict out of jail or paid his legal fees?

   ☐ Yes   ☐ No

5. Have you accepted part of the blame for the addict's behavior?

   ☐ Yes   ☐ No

6. Do you avoid talking about the addict's drinking out of fear of the response?

   ☐ Yes   ☐ No

7. Have you paid bills that the addict was supposed to have paid?

   ☐ Yes   ☐ No

8. Have you loaned the addict money?
   ☐ Yes   ☐ No

9. Have you tried drinking with the addict in hopes of strengthening the relationship?
   ☐ Yes   ☐ No

10. Have you given the addict "one more chance" and then another, and another?
    ☐ Yes   ☐ No

11. Have you threatened to leave if the addict didn't stop drinking but then did not leave?
    ☐ Yes   ☐ No

12. Have you finished a job or project that the addict failed to complete?
    ☐ Yes   ☐ No

13. Do you find yourself worrying about a person in ways that consume your time, or do you find yourself trying to come up with solutions to his problems rather than letting him do the solving?
    ☐ Yes   ☐ No

14. Do you find yourself afraid for this person, or convinced that he "cannot handle" a situation or relationship without "falling apart"?
    ☐ Yes ☐ No

15. Do you ever do something for him that he could and even should be doing?
    ☐ Yes ☐ No

16. Do you ever excuse his behavior as being a result of "stress, misunderstanding, or difficulty coping," even when the behavior hurts or inconveniences you?
    ☐ Yes ☐ No

17. Have you talked to someone for him as a way of reducing his pain?
    ☐ Yes ☐ No

18. Do you worry that you may not be doing enough for him?
    ☐ Yes ☐ No

19. Do you ever feel you have a unique and special relationship him, unlike anyone else he may know?
    ☐ Yes ☐ No

20. Do you feel protective of him - even though he is an adult and is old enough and capable of taking care of his life?
    ☐ Yes   ☐ No

21. Do you ever wish others in his life would change their behavior or attitudes to make things easier him?
    ☐ Yes   ☐ No

22. Do you feel responsible for getting him help?
    ☐ Yes   ☐ No

23. Do you feel reluctant to refer him to a source of help or assistance, uncertain if another person can understand or appreciate the addict's situation the way you do?
    ☐ Yes   ☐ No

24. Do you ever feel manipulated by this person but ignore your feelings?
    ☐ Yes   ☐ No

25. Do you ever feel that no one understands him as you do?
    ☐ Yes   ☐ No

If you answered yes to any of these questions then there is a good chance you have enabled someone in their addiction. It's time you get real and decide that you will not be complicit in their chaotic, dangerous lifestyle.

Sometimes you are too close to your situation to see how you are enabling, so we'll look at two brief case studies from my own experience to examine what enabling looks like. ✚

How Helping Becomes Enabling: Two Case Studies

I t was a late fall afternoon in the Northwest when Junior and his parents walked into my office. It's not everyday that I see people who are interested in entering our drug rehabilitation program, as we have a formal intake process for those who are struggling with addictions to methamphetamines, heroin, alcohol, prescription drugs, crack cocaine and others. Yet, occasionally I will agree to sit and talk with a family as a way of prescreening someone or as a personal favor to a friend.

I politely welcomed them into my office and ushered them to a comfortable seating area. Once the introductions were out of the way, we got down to the point of their visit.

"What can I do to help you?" I asked.

Junior's mother, Karrie, who seemed a very proper, salt-of-the-earth type of person with no affectations or pretensions, started to explain the reason for their visit. "We need help. Our son Junior has a drug problem and we want to make sure he gets the help he needs. We just don't think we have the resources to assist him anymore. We need some expert help." Karrie was expressing feelings that I have heard many times before. Having helped many addictive personalities for nearly twenty years, I understood her pain and where she was coming from on an emotional level. There is a desperation that you feel when you fear for the life of your loved one, but you don't know if you can give anymore.

They were coming to see me because their beloved son Junior was hopelessly addicted to methamphetamines and they had reached their limit. Heartbroken and confused, they had asked to speak with me regarding Junior and what they might do to help him become clean and sober.

As the leader of a non-profit agency that serves the homeless and addicted, I receive many calls from parents and spouses in this desperate situation. I have experienced people close to me - both in my family and those I've loved as friends – who have struggled with addiction. I know first hand how gut-wrenching an experience it is to watch someone you love ravaged by drugs and alcohol. I have seen the chaos that drugs wreak upon lives. This personal and professional experience has also taught me healthy ways that parents, spouses and friends of addicts can support those they love without becoming part of the problem. Too often, while trying to love and save those who are addicted, we cross the line from being helpful to being hurtful. Instead of being an encouragement and emotional support that we intended to be, we become enablers of the drug addict we are trying to help. Enablers make it possible for addicts to continue to kill themselves with drugs by assisting them in the areas of their life that are no longer functioning because of drug and alcohol abuse.

Junior and his parents were just such a case.

As Karrie continued, this became clearer. "Junior's father and I have done everything we can to help Junior, but it's not enough. We are at our wit's end with him. Could you do something to help us?"

While I sympathized with the parents, having felt these emotions myself at different times, I needed more information. What kind of drugs was Junior using? How long had he been using them? Was he ready to change? I was hoping to engage Junior to get some straight answers from him about his addiction and the scope of his problems.

Karrie spoke up quickly, "Junior's been using meth and crack for sometime now."

Junior's dad picked up from there, "He's been a real good boy and we've tried to raise him right. We go to church and have tried to example goodness to him. We just don't know where we have failed as parents."

So many parents and spouses of addicts could echo those words. There are feelings of guilt, confusion, despair, and hopelessness when dealing with someone you love who is caught up in a life of addiction. You want to do all that you can to help get back the loved one who is lost. You'd give anything to make it all better. Often parents will feel guilty for the behavior of their children. This is a common but misguided emotion. The fact is that once addicts reach an age of maturity and understanding, they are responsible for their own choices, even if that choice is drugs. These parents seemed to be doing all they could for Junior.

Junior's parents were eager to get Junior help and fully explained what had brought them to my office. Junior, they assured me, had hit bottom.

The problem with this conversation was that after a full 15 minutes of discussion, Junior hadn't said more than a word or two.

He had come in with his head hung low, trailing behind his parents, and sat quietly while his parents explained his problem and how he was ready and eager to get into treatment.

It turns out that Junior had been letting them do the talking for most of his life. They had set up an arrangement, tacitly agreed upon, that they were going to allow Junior to act in a childish and irresponsible way.

In fact, they also did a great many other things for Junior. Not only had they arranged our meeting, but they also drove him around to appointments – since he didn't have a driver's license - cooked his meals, and generally picked up after him day and night. Junior had all the markings of a spoiled little child.

Certainly a great many parents overindulge their children.

Could Karrie and her husband be that unusual? Why was I making such a critical judgment, which was perfectly clear to me at that moment, that they were enabling Junior and not helping him in any significantly positive way?

> *Well, consider this: Junior wasn't a child.*
> *Junior was 57 years old.*

Junior's parents provided a good study in enabling behavior. As I learned from our conversation and from later conversations, from the time of his earliest experiments with drugs and alcohol Junior's parents did all they could to help him. Effectively they were sheltering him from the consequences of his choices.

If he were in jail, they'd bail him out. Since he had no money they let him stay at their house, afraid that he would have nowhere to sleep. They had paid for the best rehab centers, only to have Junior drop out and head back home. When he made the slightest sign of wanting to change his life they'd kick it up a notch to reward him and life would get better for Junior. But then he'd relapse again and they'd be right back into the same cycle.

This carried on right up to the moment they walked into my office. The only reason they were there at this point, as they told me, was that they were getting too old to keep up with him.

Karrie confessed that at 85 years old, she was just concerned that there would be no one to take care of him when she died.

It was my thought at the time, and indeed I still believe this was the case, that she wanted me to step in and be his mother, but I was having none of it.

"Junior, I've heard what your mother has to say, now I'd like to hear what you have to say." I said directly. "Do *you* want to change"?

"Yes, I guess so." Junior replied meekly.

His tepid response only further reinforced the sinking feeling in my gut that Junior wasn't really invested in his own survival.

"'*I guess so*' isn't good enough, Junior. You've got to want to change. You're going to have to do the work to change, and you'll be the only one responsible for maintaining yourself in a clean and sober lifestyle. Do you want to change?"

It was tough to watch a grown man look from one parent to another searching for an answer. But that's just what he did. Junior was so conditioned to let his parents make the decisions for him that he didn't know what to do.

At that moment I knew I had to set a boundary, one that was healthy and would force Junior to make a decision to own his survival and recovery.

"I'm sorry. I don't think I can help you, Junior," I said.

Karrie and her husband were shocked. "But I thought this

was a free program, that you'd take anyone?"

I assured them that indeed our program was free, and that we didn't discriminate against anyone, but that we had *one inviolate criterion* for the program: the person had to be sick and tired of drugs. He had to *want* to change. More to the point, I told them he had to want to change for himself - that the desire of his parents wasn't enough.

But they were desperate. "Isn't there any way Junior could show you he's serious about his recovery?" Karrie turned to speak to her son, "You're serious about this, aren't you Junior?"

"Yes. I'm really serious about it," he assured her.

"Well, there is one thing you could do." I replied. "Tomorrow I'd like you to come down to our drug rehabilitation center and register for the program...by yourself. From this moment on I don't want your parents helping you get into this program. Not in any way."

There was a moment of silence.

"But Junior doesn't have a car" Karrie said softly.

"How can he get to you, if he doesn't have a car?"

"That's not your concern, Karrie. That's for Junior to figure out."

More silence.

"How about if we bring him down and he goes in by himself?" Junior's father suggested.

"No. Junior needs to do this all by himself." I held firm.

Junior sat quietly observing.

To further probe the issue I asked Junior, "When you go to buy drugs, does your mother drive you?"

"Certainly not!" He shot back, showing signs of life. "I'd never take advantage of my mother like that!"

"So you do know how to be independent when you need drugs, just not when you need recovery?"

"Well...that's different," he hesitantly answered.

But it wasn't different, and Junior eventually came to admit it. After some further conversation and convincing, he decided to come down on his own. Some days passed before Junior actually made it to the center for his intake interview with the drug counselors, but he did come on his own. He did the interview and was accepted into the program.

On the day he was scheduled to enter, however, he came pulling up with his parents just like a child being dropped off at summer camp.

His mother was quick to explain, "I know we weren't suppose to see him down here, but we couldn't let him go by himself."

I could see the writing on the wall. Junior dropped out just a few days into the program and went back to his parents home.

I still see him occasionally walking the streets, high on drugs.

Steve and Cindy had been married nearly ten years when I received a call one night out of the blue. Steve was in a total panic on the phone, saying that Cindy had taken their four-year-old son Steve Jr., and left. She had grown tired of Steve's lifestyle of addiction and chaos.

"I'm lost, David, and I don't know what to do. She's taken everything that is important to me." Steve cried over the phone.

Their road had been a bumpy one from the very beginning. Both recovered alcoholics when they met, they felt like they had finally found someone who understood their perspective on the world and that each would help make the other whole.

But according to both Steve and Cindy, what happened instead was a decade of unhealthy and enabling behavior, which culminated in a separation with both Steve and Cindy relapsing. Cindy relapsed into drinking alcohol to relieve her stress and Steve progressed to using heroin to dull his awareness of the pain he was feeling, and had caused.

It was clear to me from our conversation that Steve was strung out on drugs and that nothing I could say to him in that state would be remembered.

"The most important thing I need to know from you Steve is this…are you ready to get off of drugs and get your life back together?"

Steve insisted he was, and I arranged to have him interviewed for admission to our New Life Program at The Rescue

Mission. What unfolded in his sobriety over the next few months was a story of enabling behavior all too common.

Cindy had noticed just a few months into their marriage that Steve was withdrawing from his alcohol recovery support system and spending more time isolating from those that loved and supported him. She encouraged him to attend AA, but he always had a good excuse for not going. One week he would say he was busy, the next he would talk about how he just didn't trust the leader of the group, but the end result was the same—he was alone in his recovery.

Of course Cindy was concerned, but she loved him very much and since "No one knows Steve better than me," she believed she would see signs if he relapsed.

It wasn't too long before Steve lost his job and began to spend a lot of time working at home. Always having been an extremely independent person, Steve determined to work for himself doing odd jobs for friends and relatives. Cindy picked up the responsibility of being the main support for the family.

Arguments soon arose over money and family responsibilities, always ending with Steve storming off. These became reasons for him to take up drinking again. Cindy felt terrible for her part in shaming Steve during the arguments, and would welcome him back with open arms.

Two patterns emerged as the relationship settled into the early years. First, Cindy was the only person regularly supporting the family, and second, whatever money Steve made was for his "personal business." This "business" was often drug related and always highly speculative.

Despite what would be considered by most outside observers to be a gross inequity of responsibility, this pattern continued for the remainder of the ten years of their marriage.

One day after ten years of chaos and pain Cindy woke up to a startling revelation: *Cindy was married to and was supporting a drug dealer.*

She didn't start out her marriage with the idea of being an enabler to a drug addict, but that's exactly what happened. Everything she did was out of a *feeling* of love. She didn't *feel* right "giving up on him." Often the addicts themselves view any healthy boundary as an act of betrayal. However, Cindy wasn't giving up on Steve, she was recognizing a truth: Steve would have to make a choice between his family and his drug. By recognizing that truth and establishing a healthy boundary, Cindy was acting in honesty and love. ✚

Getting Healthy

From the outside looking in, it is easier to spot enabling behavior than if you are struggling inside a relationship. Upon reading Junior's story, most people think, "He's 57 years old! It's time for mom and dad to stop taking care of this man like he is a wayward teenager." Similarly, when you look at the relationship that Steve and Cindy developed, you can see that Cindy was clearly enabling Steve's drug lifestyle.

However, when considering our own relationships, we often have a rationale for each time we support the addict in their drug or alcoholic lifestyle. When a person allows an adult child to live with them even though that adult is using drugs, it is because, "She have no where else to go and I don't want my child living on the street." When someone else does it, we label it "Enabling." The truth is that we must get honest about our own behavior if we are to be a healthy support to our loved one who is in bondage to drugs.

My encouragement is to open your heart and mind to the possibility that your "help" may actually be prolonging the problems your friend or family member is struggling through.

By getting serious and drawing a line in the sand,
"*No more supporting habits that kill and destroy,*"
you will actually speed the arrival
of change and a new life.

Most people who are enabling an addict are absolutely certain that they are just trying to help. In their mind, they are part of the solution, not part of the problem. In reality, their help is making it easier for the addict to continue on her dangerous and destructive path. Here is the underlying motivation for us to stop enabling those we love: *If we withdraw our financial and emotional support for the addiction we will be more likely to see the person we love come to realize the destruction her abuse is causing.*

Supporting your loved one and softening the consequences of the actions she takes will certainly cause serious wreckage in her life and may ultimately kill her.

Because an addict's loved ones don't know what to do in the odd and uncertain world of drug addiction, they often fall back on doing what they 'feel' is the right thing to do. Unfortunately, feelings often lead us astray and certainly are inconsistent. If you are angry, you feel like withholding from the addict. But the next day you might feel sorry for her and worry what might happen physically, financially, or emotionally if you hold steady to your 'tough love.' You may also feel guilty about how you responded. With this new frame of mind you soften your earlier stance and 'help' the addict by giving in to the request. The cycle of addiction continues unabated.

When dealing with addicts we must not act on our feelings alone, but be armed with education and a framework for what is truly healthy and helpful for us and for the person struggling with addiction.

If you are in relationship with an addict, you need to be a student of the addiction and the addict's patterns and excuses. You need to gather knowledge on what enabling looks like and how you might be tempted to enable.

Definition of Enabling

Often I encourage a person in a relationship with an addict to commit our definition of enabling to memory, and repeat it as a reminder of how quickly assisting can become enabling.

> *Enabling is any behavior that removes or softens the consequences of addiction, thereby making it easier for the addict to continue to use drugs.*

In times of war, people have been prosecuted for what is called "giving aid and comfort to the enemy." These are any activities that would enable the enemy combatant to make war against our country. You would never want to provide financial resources to someone who was trying to kill you and destroy your country. Yet we think nothing of providing aid to a drug that is killing our loved one and destroying the person we care so much about. The very idea of "giving aid" to drugs is repulsive considering its devastating impact on our families and nation. Yet millions of people are enabling drug addicts every day and assisting in the destruction of their friend or family member. Why do we do it? Because we don't think of it as aiding a drug – a drug is an inanimate object. No, we feel we are helping a friend – making sure that no further pain comes to them and that she is protected from the consequences of her own bad decisions.

Alas, although we do it with the best of intentions, it still has the effect of prolonging the drug use of the addict and making further devastation much more likely.

But I'm just trying to help.

Enabling is often confused with helping. Parents, spouses, or friends of addicts want to help solve the problem. Just sitting by and watching your son or daughter destroy themselves is more than most parents can stand. They have to be an active participant: they want to help. I'm all for helping. Who wouldn't be? But we need to be educated about how we can best help in situations where there is addiction. When you might be crossing the line from helping to enabling, ask yourself this simple question:

> *Am I doing something for my loved one that she can and should do herself?*

If you can answer that question with a "No," then chances are you are helping her and not enabling her.

For example, let's reflect on the story of Junior. Junior's mother, Karrie, was without question enabling Junior to be a drug user. I say that because she was doing things for Junior that he could have, and certainly should have, been doing for himself, considering he was a 57 year old man.

- Paying his rent by allowing him to live in the house
- Providing food and clothing for him
- Making decisions for him
- Making excuses for his lack of motivation
- Putting words into his mouth
- Paying his debts

If Karrie had asked herself, "Am I doing something for Junior that he can or should be doing for himself?" To remain a person of honesty and integrity, I believe she would have had to say "yes."

But what could Karrie have done to help? The most important thing she could have done is to become educated about the patterns, habits and excuses of addicts. That's why it is so important that you read this book and get yourself started on the road to understanding what you must do to help save your loved one from the grip of addiction. There are many *supportive actions* Karrie could have taken, such as:

✚ **Research and get answers about options for drug treatment**. Karrie had the ability to get on the Internet and see all the information that was available about addiction, enabling, addictive substances, and potential treatments. Armed with this information, she would have an answer for Junior when he hit bottom. She would know where he could go to receive the help he needs. Often times, addicts will say, "I tried to get into rehab but they're all full" or "I can't afford rehab." Be ready with a next step on the road to recovery.

✚ **Refuse to let Junior stay in the home.** By pushing Junior out of the nest for abusing drugs and wasting his potential, Karrie would hasten the day that Junior would grow tired of his drug lifestyle. Would Junior continue to use drugs even when the financial resources and support of his parents were withdrawn? Having seen far too many of these situations, I can tell you that if an addict is willing to choose the drug over food and shelter, she is NOT ready to change and will need a very serious wake up call before she is ready to get clean and sober.

✚ **No more 'Aid and Comfort' to drugs.** Simply put, this means no more food, clothing, cars, toys, or anything else that would make the addict's life more comfortable than she would make it herself. In Junior's case, he would spend days on a drug binge and then come home to crash for a couple of days. Mom and dad provided the clothing and support. This left little motivation or even awareness in Junior to find a way out of his drug lifestyle. I have seen many situations where parents provide designer clothing to their children who are addicted to drugs so that they "don't look like a drug user." This is a dangerous game driven largely by the pride of the parent. By no longer providing this aid and comfort, your loved one will more quickly see the effects of her drug lifestyle.

✚ **Give unconditional love.** Loving someone without conditions means that you are not waiting for her to "be clean" to care for her. This is not to be confused with giving her whatever she asks for without question or stipulations. Withholding cars, clothing, and other 'stuff' from an addict is not withholding love. In fact, Karrie and her husband were doing many loving things for Junior already. They were communicating how much they cared for him. They were willing to receive him back into the good graces of the family, and they continued to believe in him. These things are all vitally necessary and important if an addict is to fight through to recovery and sobriety. If there is no hope for reconciliation with your loved ones, what's the motivation for getting better? Somewhere deep down is the young boy that Karrie and her husband love, but drugs have wreaked havoc on that boy. By believing in Junior, they can give him hope of a better future.

Similarly, in a marriage relationship that has become sick, with one spouse supporting, defending and enabling addiction, the enabler can hasten the day that the addict gets into recovery by taking a stand against their own enabling behavior.

In Steve and Cindy's situation, she was enabling him for many years by providing him with aid and comfort he needed to run his illicit business and maintain his drug habit. Fearful that she would lose the family that she had always dreamed of, and conflicted by her belief in the importance of marriage, she was extremely reluctant to draw any firm boundary that would push Steve away.

Many spouses tolerate dangerous and unhealthy behavior for what seem to be good reasons, but are actually deeply rooted dysfunctions. In their effort to keep the family together, they often pass on the family dysfunction to another generation, as the children watch what happens and repeat it when they become adults. Spouses sometimes feel they are in a double bind. If they kick the addict or abuser out they will be sinning against God, bringing an end to their marriage. However, if they stay in an abusive marriage they will be miserable and in danger. There is no win.

However, there are alternate scenarios and you must not allow yourself the self-pity of double-bind thinking. What if leaving your addicted spouse forces her to see the error of her ways and seek treatment? If a spouse or parent is in physical danger and under the threat of abuse they should not hesitate to get into a safe place. Perhaps separating your children from the madness of an addictive lifestyle will help them develop in a healthier environment. They don't have to repeat the same mistakes as their parent, but if they are left in that chaotic environment, they most certainly will. Many times the addict is intentionally forcing the spouse to make a decision.

There is an expectation that the non-addicted spouse will have to make all the hard choices. This situation is untenable and incredibly unfair to the spouse who is left with these choices. When this happens, I encourage the spouse to consider the addict's actions as a decision in itself. The addict has chosen the drug over the marriage, and that is a decision.

In Cindy's case, this is exactly what happened. Steve loved the idea of family, but had really chosen his habit over Cindy and the kids. It was only when she cut off this support that Steve was forced to make a decision: He could either find another enabling relationship or he could decide to get the help he needed.

When faced with these two decisions, many addicts will quickly move in with other friends or relatives who will enable them to continue to use and abuse. That is why the section on *Unity* is a must-read for families battling this problem. Many spouses fear that when given a choice, the addict will choose to get another enabling relationship and they will lose their marriage. This must be acknowledged as a real possibility. But the alternatives are even starker. Spouses who enable addictive behaviors are killing their chances for future happiness and a healthy home. There is almost no chance that the addict will change without the spouse forcing them to make a decision between the drug and their relationship.

There are legions of other stories of successful outcomes from spouses who identify that they are in enabling relationships and then make a concerted decision to draw a line in the sand.

In the case of Cindy and Steve, she asked Steve to move out. Cindy set boundaries and expectations that Steve would need to get into treatment and reshape his life before she would consider any reconciliation. Steve reached out for help and got into treatment, and slowly, his life began to get back on track.

> *Drawing the line on his behavior was ultimately the best thing Cindy could have done for him.*

Don't give up hope. Many times it takes a separation or even a divorce to force an addictive spouse to see that drugs have destroyed their life. In the end, it is important to remember that these are life and death situations. There aren't a lot of aged meth addicts or crack addicts. That's because they either change, or they die. If a divorce is what it takes to save someone's life, then it should be considered as an option.

Often, addicts will snap out of their addictive pattern when it becomes clear that they will risk losing the love and support of those closest to them because of their addiction. ✚

Ten Treatments for Enabling

Now that you understand what enabling really is, and you recognize that you are unknowingly contributing to keeping the addictive lifestyle alive, it's time to learn what positive steps you can take to rebuild healthy boundaries and begin creating an environment where everything is pushing your loved one towards recovery.

Addiction and the chaotic mess that results is a new world to many. With the variety and accessibility of inexpensive drugs growing in the past thirty years, we have seen an explosion of drug problems and their related societal consequences. Crime, divorce, bankruptcy, single parent households, teen pregnancy, truancy, juvenile crime and many other issues we are dealing with in our communities are directly related to the increase of drug and alcohol addiction.

Parents, know the signs of drug usage.

Even with its invasion of our homes and families, many of us don't have the slightest clue how to recognize the signs of abuse and how to help the addict get back on the road to a healthy, productive life. Many parents mistakenly believe that drugs and alcohol are an assumed fact of life and therefore overlook the serious abuse that is taking place in their homes. They excuse behaviors that are signals of drug abuse until it's too late. Because they don't know the difference between teenage rebellion and signs of drug usage, they are caught unaware.

Of course, parenting teens is a difficult task with the changes in mood and behavior that are typical of every child as they develop into adulthood. Yet there are some signs, when seen together or as a series of behaviors, which are clues to drug use.

- Change in friends
- Teen is verbally or physically abusive
- Sudden increase or decrease in appetite
- Valuable items or money disappear
- Not coming home on time
- Not telling you where he is going
- Constant excuses for behavior
- Spending a lot of time in his room
- Lies about activities
- Finding the following: cigarette rolling papers, pipes,

roach clips, small glass vials, plastic baggies, remnants of drugs (seeds, etc.)
- Sudden drop in grades
- Truancy
- Loss of interest in learning
- Sleeping in class
- Poor work performance
- Not doing homework
- Defiant of authority
- Poor attitude towards sports or other extracurricular activities previously enjoyed
- Reduced memory and attention span
- Irritable, "Edgy"
- Decrease/increase/sporadic appetite

Friends, spouses and co-workers should know the signs of drugs, too!

It's not just parents of teens who need to know the signs of serious drug use. If you are in a position to be an enabler in the life of the addict, then you need to be informed so that you know you are not contributing to addiction.

Fortunately, information is available online about alcohol, meth, cocaine, heroin, prescription drug abuse and more. What are the signs that you might look for in a coworker or adult loved one that might, if taken as a whole, possibly indicate drug use?

- Withdrawal
- Depression
- Criminal behavior
- Frequent need of money
- Excessive sleeping
- Unusual energy
- Erratic behavior
- Difficulty at work
- Suspicious friendships

These are all common signs of drug use in both adults and teens.

Excuses, Excuses

It's not just the signs of drug abuse that you must learn to observe, you must also know the common excuses and evasive maneuvers addicts use when they are trying to minimize or deny their behaviors. Sometimes I hear parents say, "My child would never lie to me. We have a very close relationship." While I'm in no position to question the *honesty* of their relationship with their child, my experience has taught me that 100% of addicts will lie and misdirect in order to keep from getting caught in their abuse, or will minimize their abuse.

Of course, this kind of betrayal often hurts more than any financial or real property loss you might suffer through theft. It cuts right to the nature of the relationship: Trust. Let me give you a bit of encouragement, no matter how hollow it may sound. *Your loved one, under the incredible pull of chemical dependency, will say anything to be free from observation and critical judgment. It truly is the drug talking.* Once your loved one is free from chemical addiction, he will likely feel great remorse for the lies he has told.

As you walk this path of freedom from enabling the addict, you must have healthy skepticism about every excuse and explanation the addict is giving you to explain erratic behavior. Fortunately, even though the addict will feel like he is giving you a completely original answer, there are patterns and commonalities between addicts and their excuses that make it much easier to spot the half-truths and outright lies.

Such statements as, "I can quit anytime I want," "I'm not as bad as other people," and "Everybody is doing it," are common and well-known excuses. There are, however, more complicated excuses for erratic behavior that addicts fabricate in order to make you believe they are not using.

Why were they out all night? "My car broke down and I had to go to Jimmy's house. He didn't have his license and you know how paranoid he is about driving without his license, so we decided to wait until his dad got home. Jimmy's dad is out of town on business, so I had to spend the night. Call Jimmy if you want to follow up on me."

When faced with such stories you should feel no responsibility to track down and verify the information. Responsible adults find ways to communicate with each other and to make sure that misunderstandings are minimal. Of course, parents of teenagers can expect a different level of accountability and transparency than a peer-to-peer, adult relationship. Your expectation should be that the addict or suspected addict should show reasonable effort to communicate with you. Most serious addicts will not be able to keep any but the simplest promises, and you need only be patient until the situation becomes clear. Missing appointments, erratic behavior, unstable job performance and large periods of unaccounted-for time will bring excuses and lies to buffer the consequences of these actions.

Do not be tempted to accept and excuse such behaviors in order to maintain relationships. Yet the loss of your trust could be one of the important consequences that would snap the addict back into reality.

Let the addict know that you seriously question his behavior and the validity of his statements. If he doesn't act in a way that shows respect for you, then you will lose trust in him (although you continue to love him). This is very difficult medicine for both the addict and the enabler. Yet until you draw a boundary in regard to honesty and excuses, you will continue enabling the erratic behavior that could kill your loved one. This is serious business—not something to be laughed at. Do not minimize the silly and transparent excuses.

✚ 2. Communicate unconditional love.

These Treatments will require you to use discipline, firm resolve and follow-through to hold the line on the unusual and erratic behavior of the addict you love. However, without your ability to communicate unconditional love in the midst of these 'tough love' actions, you will feel unbalanced in your approach and will likely lose the resolve to follow through. Enablers are often motivated by a need to protect and nurture. Tough love doesn't seem like a viable option to these personality types. *Regularly reaffirming your unconditional love will reassure yourself that you are communicating love to the addict.*

This is important because the addict *will not* see your actions as helpful. In fact, you will be accused of being unloving and unsupportive. Since giving resources, money and logistical support to an addict is enabling behavior, you must no longer do these things. You must rely upon verbally affirming your love. This will seem insufficient to the addict since all he wants is the money and freedom to continue in his destructive path. Do not allow yourself to be persuaded that what you are doing is unloving. In the long-term, what you are doing is contributing to, and speeding the arrival of, the day the addict seeks help by allowing the addict to feel the consequences of his choices.

Saying words like:

- "I know it doesn't seem like it right now, but I love you very much and want you to get the help you need."
- "I love you very much, but I also know that love doesn't mean telling you everything you want to hear."
- "I'll always love you but I can't contribute to you killing yourself."

These are all phrases that let the addict know you are serious and that you want to express love to him.

Verbally communicating unconditional love is not natural to many people, so it must be something that you consciously plan to articulate. Some people have a hard time expressing any emotion. Others have a habit of making conditional statements of support. Know yourself, and the impression you seek to give to the addict. If you consistently have taken the role of enforcer and boundary keeper, you will need to train yourself to communicate your love verbally or risk further alienating your loved one. Conversely, if you are naturally good at communicating love but have a tough time keeping healthy boundaries, you will need to learn sensible and life-saving boundaries.

In either situation, it is critical to be unconditional in your love. The addict will disappoint you and try to manipulate you. In the long-term, your unconditional love will mean all the difference to the addict in rebuilding his life and seeking people he can trust to give him the healthy support he needs.

Many enablers misunderstand healthy support and unconditionally assist the addict in keeping the addiction alive and holding the massive complications and consequences of that addiction at bay. One parent that I spoke with wanted to help his daughter and son-in-law, deep in the grips of meth addiction, get off drugs and rebuild their lives. Their addictive lifestyle had caught the attention of the law, and the couple escaped to Canada to avoid prosecution. This normally rational parent, in the name of unconditional love, concocted a plan to sneak them back into the country. He set up a prescribed drop time when the couple could sneak across a field into the United States, where the father would be waiting. As soon as the addicts reached this country, they were set up in a hotel for the night, on the father's dime. They began using again and dropped out of sight for an additional two years. This father now sees that his actions were not helpful, but indeed aided the addicts in their disease.

Instead of an unquestioning, naïve enabling, *we need to love unconditionally and support through verbal affirmation.* Truly, it is difficult to imagine how we could over-communicate to addicts that we love them, while not assisting them in the addictions that are ruining their lives.

✚ 3. Refuse to give financial & resource support.

Enablers differ from each other in many ways: gender, age, socioeconomic factors and more, however in this way all enablers are the same: They all give financial, resource and logistical support to the addict they love.

> *Best intentions aside, this logistical support is directly tied to an addict's ability to support a chaotic lifestyle, centered on chemical addiction.*

Without the financial support of the enablers in his life, the addict will quickly run out of money and resources with which to keep the illusion of a manageable lifestyle. With his spouse, parents or friends paying his bills and covering his losses, he can imagine that he is keeping it all together. Unfortunately, this illusion is dangerous to the addict, emboldening him to keep pursuing the good life that drugs promise, but never deliver. He will travel deeper into the addiction.

But it's not just cash that fuels a drug addict's lifestyle; it is also the use of other tangible assets. Providing him with gas, food, the use of a car, and free housing are all examples of how people provide enabling resources to an addict. Simply put, if an addict can receive housing with little or no cost, then he have more cash resources to pour into his addiction.

Clearly the concern that their loved one would end up hungry and homeless drives many enablers to justify their financial and resource support of the addict. "No son of mine will be living on the street," is a common statement from the parent of the addict. I've also heard statements such as, "I don't want my daughter to look like a drug addict, so I buy her all the new clothes she needs." These types of enabling behaviors are rooted in foolish and deadly pride.

Reminder: Enabling is any behavior that removes or softens the consequences of addiction, thereby making it easier for the addict to continue to use drugs.

Financial support, the giving of resources and logistical support of the drug addict will make the problem worse and prolong the day of his recovery. Often the enabler is so close to the situation and so enmeshed in an unhealthy codependence with the addict they can't see the illogical and counterproductive nature of their enabling behavior.

Imagine this true-life scenario I encountered. Two loving parents insisted on providing housing and name brand clothing for their beautiful daughter while she struggled with a serious chemical addiction. The rationale for their support was that without their support she would have to live in drug houses and perhaps prostitute herself to support her habit. They couldn't bear to imagine this scenario for their little girl. As is usually the case in enabling relationships, the justification for the enabling behavior helped to facilitate the actual situation they were seeking to avoid.

Fast-forward six years later—their daughter has maintained a room in the house and a closet full of clothes, but she spends time there only between binges at drug houses. She now has an extensive criminal record and has been involved in all the painful situations the parents wished to spare her. By providing a soft landing whenever she ran out of resources, the parents literally enabled their daughter to continue her chemical abuse for six additional years. Only recently the parents have begun to realize their role in her addiction and, upon this realization, withdrew their support. Almost immediately she hit bottom, entered a drug rehab program and got on the road to recovery. While there are no guarantees, it is highly likely that their daughter would have hit bottom sooner and entered rehab if they had withdrawn their financial, resource and logistical support six years earlier.

This case is not uncommon. In fact, most people get serious about cutting off resource support only after an addiction is full blown and has been maintained for some time. Often, they wait until they cannot afford to support the addict any longer. In this way, wealthy families have a built in disadvantage, because they can financially afford to enable the addict in perpetuity. Still, they should consider that withdrawing financial support may speed the day of their loved one's recovery.

Ask yourself these important questions:

Q: If addicts will not change when you stop paying their bills, under what conditions would your disapproval get them to see the light?

A: None. If the addict does not change when support is withdrawn, then he would not have changed with support in place.

Q: If the addict is willing to lose everything in order to maintain addiction, is there anything you can do to stop him?

A: No. An addict will continue destroying himself until he is sick and tired of the addiction. Enabling support makes sure this day will never come.

Q: Is there any aid and comfort that would make an addict see the errors of his ways?

A: No. Enablers give aid and comfort as a show of 'love' to the addict. Addicts use this aid to further medicate, in effect manipulating the enabler.

Q: Are addicts likely to change if you reward their chaotic behavior with cash, housing and logistical support?

A: Absolutely not.

While these questions may seem harsh to some, they are in fact exactly the clear-minded questions you must ask yourself.

First-Aid Treatment means doing the following:

✚ Cut off all financial support to the addict.
Parents of teens will need to use sober judgment when deciding on how to best support the child, keeping the definition of enabling in mind at all times.

✚ Do not provide housing for the addict.

Statements like, "As long as you are using drugs we cannot live together," and "We won't support you in your drug habit by paying your rent," are statements that can help you draw the line. As an enabler, you may be too close to see how allowing the addict to live with you hurts the addict; but it is allowing him logistical support so that he can use the drug. A spouse can and should consider asking the addicted spouse to leave the house. In all cases, caution and safety should be considered when these conversations are taking place. Addicts can become violent when the walls of their world start to crumble around them. This sign of panic is often a clue that you are nearing a break-though. If your child is under the age of 18, it is perfectly appropriate to allow them to stay in the house, if they are willing to accept boundaries that will help to build trust and ensure a safe environment.

✚ Be in Unity.

If the father of an addict ceases enabling behaviors, but the mother continues to give the addict the resources he needs to sustain his lifestyle, then progress will be impossible. In fact, disunity between parents on this issue could well pull your family and marriage apart. Likewise, parents who are in unity but who fail to educate grandparents, siblings, and friends of the addict will also struggle to see progress. While the addict may normally have the most charming and self-less of personalities; when they are controlled by addiction, the appetite for drugs overrides the personality you have come to trust. The addict becomes a manipulator who will go around the parents to the grandparents if possible. ***Stay in unity.*** Of course, the addict can always go to drug-related friendships, but it is likely that these relationships will be less satisfying and supportive and will not sustain long-term enabling support.

✚ Communicate to the addict that the support system is united on the need for recovery.

The addict works one family member against another. When one friend closes the enabling door, there is often another who will open an enabling window. It is important to let the addict know that you've been talking with folks, and that you'll not be outflanked in your efforts to help him get clean and sober.

Making a phone call to another family member or friend is often very difficult, as they may be at a totally different stage of understanding than you are about the addiction. For example, recently I was talking with a woman who had struggled with her husband's alcohol addiction for at least a decade. When she began to set healthy boundaries in their relationship, she decided to call his parents to discuss the situation. Unfortunately, they were either totally unaware of the problem or had been denying it to themselves, and they offered her little support.

For this reason, it is good to consider how you can help others process the information that you are giving them. Understandably, many people in crisis are so desperate to be heard that they do an information dump on anyone who will listen. While it's important to communicate with an addict's support system, not everyone will need to know all of the information you have, and they will certainly need to process and assimilate what is happening.

Nevertheless, it's critical to surround your loved one, to the degree possible, with people who will act in healthy ways and support the addict in seeking recovery. This is only possible through communication.

✚ Allow the addict to seek public assistance.

Many people shudder to think of their loved one at a homeless shelter or going to a soup kitchen for food. But the reality is this helps many addicts realize how far they have fallen. Having seen many Rescue Missions and shelters, I know that most are prepared to give the support your loved one needs without enabling and rewarding bad behavior. In most cases, an addict will hit bottom well before they are in serious danger of becoming chronically homeless or starving to death. In most American cities, this is an illogical fear. Your loved one needs to face the depth of his addiction. If allowed to feel even a little bit of the consequences of their behavior, they may well seek recovery. The fact that many addicts insist that they're 'better than' drug addicts and those who are in homeless shelters, only reinforces the point. They aren't better; *they are exactly the same*. Dangerous pride pervades the lives of people who are toying with addiction; especially those who have the means to continue living comfortably while enslaved to their drug. They need to awaken to the fact that addiction leads to a loss of relationship, resources, freedom, health and shelter.

✚ 4. Be truthful about the addict's behavior.

While it is perfectly natural to want to protect the

reputation of your loved one, you cannot keep secrets that will slow the process of addressing the addiction. If the addict is acting erratically due to chemical dependency, then you need to be honest about that fact when asked by friends and family members. This will create positive peer pressure to address the problem. Sometimes families will keep these addictions secret for years, believing that they are somehow saving the reputation of the addict. Unfortunately, the addict's behavior will be much more damaging to his reputation than a public confirmation of addiction.

Recently, I visited with a mother, Sonja, who had a son struggling with addiction. Her son was in his mid-forties and had lost his job, family and health to addiction. He had been honest with his brother and admitted his addiction to prescription drugs, and then his brother had done the right thing and informed the family. After learning of this development, Sonja had come to me looking for answers as to how she could help her son to get healthy. However, as soon as we sat down to discuss the matter, she began to make excuses for her son's behavior and even denied that he had any problem at all. At one point in the conversation, I asked her, "If you don't believe he has a problem, why are you here and what do you suppose I can do for you?"

Such is the nature of family dynamics and denial. Often the matter of denial and cover up is so ingrained that even when you are absolutely sure the person you love has a problem, you are also at the same time covering it up, lying to yourself and others about it. Although Sonja knew in one part of her mind that her son was addicted, she was denying it publically and making excuses for her son's behavior. Several times each week, she took her son to medical appointments so that he could get more prescription drugs. When one doctor refused to give him more, she would take him to another doctor. She was helping him doctor shop, a common enabling habit among those supporting an addict to pain medications.

> *Enablers must fight the urge to make excuses*
> *and cover up for the addict.*

The addict lives in a world of denial, blame, minimizing and distortion. It is a temptation for the enabler to be drawn into that world. Truth, educated assumptions, and firm boundaries are the only weapons you may have to fight this temptation. Is there ever a circumstance when you may need to withhold information from others? Perhaps, but in my experience this is not the problem of enablers. Enablers always find reasons to withhold truth and live in a fantasy world the addict has created. Discipline yourself to live in reality, no matter how painful that reality might be. It is the only way to get to real solutions.

✚ 5. Hold the addict accountable for broken promises.

Addicts have many regrets and much unfinished business in their lives. Eventually, the sum total of these actions will become overwhelming. It is easy for an enabling personality to excuse actions and push them into the past. Enablers don't want to bring up painful memories or in any way push the addict away. However, it is critical that an addict understands the chaos and unresolved issues that he leaves in his wake.

Most of us are familiar with the phrase, "don't kick a guy when he's down," and few people like holding someone accountable for their past promises and words. It is somehow not good form. While I would not encourage you to continually throw someone's own words in their face—especially words or promises made during years of drug use—neither is it healthy to pretend as though these things were never said.

A father struggling with addiction may make promises to his children that he doesn't follow through on when under the influence of the drug. When he finally emerges from his stupor he will be ready and willing to turn a new page in his life. However, an important part of truly responsible behavior is facing up to the words said and actions taken while under the influence.

Typically, in our rush to welcome an addict back, we short circuit the recovery process by cleaning up the mess left behind or ignoring the mess altogether.

A healthy balance requires acknowledgement of past mistakes and a willingness to make amends for those mistakes.

✚ 6. Follow through; don't threaten.

It's likely that all of us, at one time or another, have seen the frustrating and sometimes humorous scene of a parent negotiating with a petulant child in a public place such as a grocery store or shopping mall. While the child is throwing a very public tantrum, the parent threatens to withhold something from the child or punish the child in some way. Often, the child knows better than the rest of the onlookers that the parent isn't really going to follow through with the threats, so he continues the tantrum until the parent gives in.

A friend of mine who served as a law enforcement officer once told me that policemen are trained to either give a ticket for speeding, or give a lecture, but not both. People don't want both a lecture and a punishment—it goes against human nature. In the same way, we shouldn't enforce a punishment and then give a lecture, that's a double punishment; and piling-on causes the addict to withdraw.

Dealing with an addict in a healthy, loving way will require you and others to be firm and consistent in your boundaries, standards, assistance and encouragement. Nothing undermines the process of recovery from enabling more than threatening harsh and severe steps without the follow-through to back it up. It clearly sends a message to the addict that you are not consistent and if he hangs in there, he will be bailed out once again.

Often the challenge of being consistent is made even more difficult by the fact that these dramas play out over months and even years. If this is the case, what can you do to help yourself and others who love the addict to be consistent?

First, understand that you can't make the addict well. Even by withholding and punishing the addict, you are not able to make him come to the realization that the drug is destroying his life, hurting those around him, and causing chaos that is making his life difficult. Unless you understand and accept this you will be lulled into believing that, if you pick just the right punishment, you will be able to jolt the addict out of his destructive behavior. This savior mentality feeds the enabling process. The healthy mindset is to realize that only the addict can make the choice of recovery and that it is ultimately between the addict and God. By holding tight to this realization, you can free yourself from the feeling of being responsible to provide the financial and logistical support that coddles addiction.

When you realize that you cannot make the addict be healthy, you will not feel the need to threaten consequences that you will later, in quiet moments of reflection, regret you made or be tempted to retreat on.

You will need to set some *healthy boundaries* that are

clearly articulated. I even suggest writing these boundaries down, either for your own remembrance, or to communicate clearly to the addict. Healthy boundaries include things like the following:

- I will always love and accept my loved one who is struggling with addiction.
- I will verbally remind him of my love.
- I will recommend treatments and programs to get free.
- I will not provide money when he is in his addiction so that he will have more resources to buy the drug.
- I will not provide him with housing so that he can use his other resources to buy drugs and live a lifestyle that will kill him.
- I will not keep his secrets and aid him in living a double life.
- I will not run errands, make phone calls, and make excuses in order to clean up the he is making under the influence of the addiction.
- I will do everything I can to be spiritually strong for others and myself.

There are undoubtedly more boundaries and affirmations to help us realize where we need to stay firm and where we can offer assistance that will actually help the addict, instead of assisting him to go deeper into his chaotic lifestyle.

Instead of threatening to take severe action, give careful thought, rooted in a healthy understanding of what role you can play in encouraging and loving the addict, *before* you set boundaries. Threatening quickly falls into the category of "overpromising and under delivering" when you speak in haste and don't have the benefit of education and forethought.

✚ 7. Extend loving words of encouragement.

How important it is too continue to verbalize the love and encouragement that we all need! All to often we withhold our approval, waiting for people to meet our tough standards before we will give them our love. This is never healthy, and we should always strive to verbalize our feelings, as unnatural as it may seem to many of us. Dealing with the potential loss of a loved one due to addiction is often the rude awakening we need to realize that we have become closed in our emotional support of the addict, under the misunderstanding that verbalizing love would be seen as a sign of support for their destructive behavior.

Literally flipping healthy behavior upside down, we withhold the verbal support and loving affirmations of the individual, and give him money and logistical support to compensate for our guilty feelings and sense of responsibility. Instead, we should make a regular habit of telling and reminding the addict that he is loved. We should also explain that we are ready to help him connect with treatment when he is ready, but that we will not give physical or financial assistance as long as he is killing himself.

It is totally possible that this important distinction will be lost on the addict, who will much prefer to have your money than assurances of undying love. Yet it is just this sort of crucial distinction that will, in the end, help to create healing and a healthy result should the addict decide to seek help.

Most typically, we try to badger or argue with the addict in order to get him to wake up to his destructive behavior. But badgering seldom works and puts you in an emotionally unhealthy place, one in which you will have a hard time being supportive once the addict actually does begin to make healthy choices.

✚ 8. Be ready with next steps & solutions.

It can be a helpless feeling to watch someone you love going through the pain and anguish of addiction. It has been said that addiction is when you can't get enough of something you don't want. And so it is. For those watching from the outside, often especially for mothers, it can seem more than you can bear. You desperately want to do something, anything, to help your child get out of the grips of this terrible drug. Now here you are hearing that there is precious little you can do in a practical sense to relieve, assist, or support him in his struggle.

Nevertheless, we must be committed to doing whatever we must do to create an environment where the addict feels the full weight of his mistakes as soon as possible, so as to create an atmosphere where he is most likely to grow tired of the fallout of his addiction and seek recovery. If we keep the addict from experiences or consequences of addiction by providing logistical and financial support, we postpone his eventual awakening to his true situation and to seeking recovery.

Parents, spouses, friends and loved ones should take seriously the role of becoming a student of the addiction and strive to learn all they can about the drug, its effects, and potential programs and support groups for both the addict and the loved one.

Take the time to research programs such as Alcoholics Anonymous, Narcotics Anonymous, Al-Anon, Celebrate Recovery, the local Salvation Army and Rescue Mission to find out what might work best for the addict and how you can get support to stay strong spiritually and emotionally.

There are also an abundance of good books and websites on addiction and specific drugs with which you should familiarize yourself.

✚ 9. Look for teachable moments.

Even if it doesn't feel natural to do so, imagine taking the healthy steps to create an environment where the addict will come to a personal realization of his state of addiction. Affirm that you have healthy boundaries; you have educated yourself about the addiction, and your role in loving and encouraging the individual who is in the grips of the addiction. You will not be emotionally drawn into the chaos and drama of the addict. Instead, you will work hard to be spiritually healthy and emotionally stable. Doing what you must do to make yourself healthy.

Now what?

Once the important steps of healthy behavior have been taken and are being maintained, you need to look for teachable moments in the life of the addict. In many cases, the addict may not even remember the long talks and lectures that you gave while he was intoxicated or high; much of what you think you have communicated may have been lost on the loved one. Continue to look for moments of breakthrough in understanding, when the addict is broken, hurting, needing comfort or is seemingly clean and sober. At these moments, reinforce the love you have for him. Don't change or loosen your healthy boundaries, as this may encourage a return to manipulation. Instead, give him the love, encouragement, and information you have that will help him get into treatment. It might sound something like this: "I love you and want to see you get healthy. I've found out there are programs that can help you get clean and sober. I really hope you'll make an effort to get into a program when you're ready. They have an opening right now." Or you might say, "There is an AA class at the church on Thursday nights at 7. If you're ready to listen and realize where this addiction has taken you, I think they could help."

Looking for teachable moments means realizing when the addict is open to hearing from you. Addiction is often characterized by isolating from those who are healthy and will speak truth into the life of the addict, so it is important to be looking for those moments when the addict is open to hearing the truth. Teachable moments are not a time for you to give in to requests for money or assistance, but are times to connect addicts with the tools and programs that can help him should he decide to get well. You can't make him be healthy. If you try to be the savior of his life, you will only prolong the problem and postpone the day he hits bottom.

✚ 10. Be patient and consistent.

All this healthy behavior requires patience, often more than we think we possess. That is why it is so critically important to focus on your behavior, doing the things that you know will help you to be healthy physically, emotionally, and spiritually. As long as you focus on those things that only you can control, you will be making progress. In order to recover the addict will need to take important steps. You must be willing to let that person go through his journey, no matter how painful, in order to come out the other side healthy. If your loved one is not willing to get free from his addiction in the face of financial ruin, jail time, and loss of relationship, will they ever come to recovery when you are financially, logistically, and emotionally running interference? You are buffering him from the consequences that will wake him from denial. By no longer enabling him, you allow him to feel the full weight and consequences of his decisions. You are doing it to save his life.

Once again, being in unity with others in your boundaries and having a support group of others going through the same challenges will help you to develop the perspective and education that you will need. Stay patient and prayerful in your journey to help your loved one who is struggling with addiction. ✚

6

What Happens When You Stop Enabling?

One evening after I gave a speech to a group of parents, who had children struggling with addiction, a woman came up to me and asked a question. Her name was Sally, and she had patiently waited until other parents had asked their questions and there were just a few folks milling around. Apparently, she had waited because she was nervous to address me when anyone else was within earshot. Sally's question was troubling.

She quietly whispered her question to me, "What do I do if I'm physically or emotionally attacked when I set up new boundaries?"

As I was filled in on her circumstances, it became clear that Sally was in a desperately difficult situation. She explained that both of her sons, grown men, had been living with her for some time and had turned her home into a drug den. She was living every day in fear. Initially Sally had invited the boys back home in order to help them, but this quickly became an enabling situation that escalated out of control.

Now she was literally a prisoner in her own home, and the very thought of beginning to put down firm boundaries, which she recognized was necessary, was very scary, indeed.

In Sally's situation, we needed to support her by coordinating law enforcement and using the law to her advantage, literally reporting her son's crimes and having the police escort the boys out of the house. Many other parents do not fear physical danger, but rather fear losing relationship with their loved one.

Healthy relationships require consistently good decisions and nurturing. Just as a garden doesn't grow into a beautiful, orderly array of colors, shapes and varieties without the care of a gardener, so it is with a relationship with your loved one. You must make decisions on how this relationship can best develop. Often these are hard and difficult decisions.

The first step, which we've discussed in earlier chapters, is realizing the ways in which you protect your loved one from the consequences of her behavior. You need to identify the ways in which you may be enabling her. The next step is to establish firm boundaries, zero financial assistance, along with overwhelming verbal and emotional support. You need to find a safe and direct way to stop the enabling behavior and to communicate loving support without interjecting yourself into the problems, lifestyle and drama that exist in the life of the addict.

Once you have identified and confronted the problem,

you can begin to rebuild a healthier pattern of support and love that will empower you and play an important role in encouraging the addict to make a decision as to whether or not she will seek help for her sickness.

Why You Must Take a Stand Against the Addiction

Enabling relationships are unhealthy. Enabling involves carrying the weight of responsibility for another capable adult. It may consist of covering her expenses, hiding transgressions, or making sure she won't lose her job. This encourages an addict's chaotic patterns and drug-fueled lifestyle, which is not balanced and healthy for either of you. To establish balance and health in a relationship with a drug user requires some seemingly simple steps, but is probably one of the most difficult things you will ever have to do in your lifetime.

Enabling behavior is ultimately only rewarding in the short term. By paying someone's bills you are saving her from her present trouble. However, that enabling behavior will create a pattern of long-term behaviors that will wear you down and further encourage drug-related activities. Many times, enabling behavior is described as codependency. Codependency is when both people get a benefit from unhealthy behavior. Enablers often feel like they are the "fixer" coming to the rescue of their good friend. Thoughts of self-satisfaction often fill the mind of the enabler. "What would she do without me?" "I'm the only person who understands." "I'm the only one she trusts." "I'm still needed by my child." These are all common thoughts of codependent enablers. Have you ever considered the ways you might be benefiting emotionally from enabling this person's behavior? These are thoughts that will justify behavior that is rewarding in the short-term but that reinforce the drug habit. To break the cycle of addiction and enabling addiction, we have to make tough, heart-wrenching decisions.

Healthy behavior with an addict is long-term based, and you need to know there are no short cuts to recovery. When you draw the line in the sand, some addicts quickly get the message and begin to consider the impact their behavior has had and the road on which addiction has take them. With this new reality they decide to change and seek a clean and sober lifestyle. Many addicts, however, will not have this awareness. It will take many addicts a multitude of painful lessons before they will reach bottom.

Instead of turning around and heading towards sobriety and a great new life, an addict may turn on you and try to make your behavior the issue.

As with any new endeavor, you'll need a game plan for success. In my experience, if you have not worked out what your boundaries will be, and have not gotten the support you need to hold a consistent boundary, you'll never follow through.

For this reason I recommend the following:

✚ **Decide on Healthy Boundaries Before Speaking with the Addict.** Oftentimes people make snap judgments and impulsive statements under the pressure of an argument, or because they've reached a breaking point under duress. Later, when the addict has sobered up and apologized, or the pressure has subsided, the enabler recants earlier boundary statements and the cycle begins again. Instead of repeating this negative pattern over and over again, make a list of healthy boundaries, before you have a big conversation.

✚ **Set Boundaries in Consultation.** Disunity within the family, with one parent setting reasonable boundaries and the other continuing to enable addiction, is never going to be optimum. Unfortunately, it can sometimes be very difficult to get the entire support system to set healthy boundaries. Nevertheless, you must determine to have healthy boundaries regardless of what others do or say. It is still critically important to consult and communicate with everyone who may be affected by your new, healthy values.

✚ **Always Create a Safe Environment for Addressing Issues.** Sally (referred to at the beginning of this chapter) needed to literally bring law enforcement to support her new boundaries. In most cases, this isn't necessary. Unfortunately, with the high rates of spousal abuse, you must think of all potential eventualities when you are ready to address this issue head on. Be cautious and prepared. Changing locks, security codes and implementing other safety measures should all be considered. It shows a seriousness of resolve and will be a precaution to keep you safe when confronting the unpredictable addict.

Here are the common defenses that you will see when you begin to make healthier decisions:

- *Denial.* When confronted with the painful reality of their addiction, many addicts will flat out deny the problem. This is true even if that person has at other points admitted they have an addiction problem. Past statements, facts and reality will not stop an addict from living in denial. Many people know internally that their alcohol use has become a problem, but will steadfastly deny it to you. This inconsistency should not cause you to doubt what you have experienced and know to be true. You are not responsible for the addict accepting your new relationship boundaries; you are only responsible for your own decisions.

- *Isolation.* When confronted by healthy boundaries and the removal of enabling systems, many addicts choose to isolate themselves. Just as small children will slam the door and pout in their rooms when they don't get ice cream for dinner, so an addict will withdraw from you when you refuse to pay their rent or lie on her behalf. If your family is in unity in this endeavor to help the addict, it is likely that the addict will isolate from the entire group and choose to associate with people who approve of addictive behavior or give in to her demands. A loved one withdrawing from you for any reason is painful, but this is especially true for parents and spouses of an addict. You have always imagined a life in harmony with this person, and now it seems as though you are driving her away. In fact, this may just be the accusation that the addict makes. In truth, however, you are making a decision to be the firm foundation of the family. By communicating unconditional love and being prepared with solutions the addict can take when ready, you can steel your resolve against such accusations. Nevertheless, you must be prepared to allow the person to withdraw from you and not give in to her demands.

- *Rationalizing.* Addicts will often rationalize their destructive behavior when under pressure and when the facts are stacked against them. "I've been under a lot of pressure lately so I've been drinking to relax" and other excuses are common when a person is faced with the unforgiving truth. Often, this will be personally directed at you. Since in the mind of the addict you are the one causing the pain by withholding the enabling support she craves, you will be an implied, if not explicit, target of such rationalizing statements. An addict may want to give you reasons why she drinks or uses drugs in order to soften your perception of her behavior but this doesn't change the reality. You must be committed to living in reality. By taking the healthy steps of educating yourself about these excuses and holding the addict responsible for her behavior you will be prepared to withstand this diversion.

- *Blaming.* Blaming is the gold standard of addictive behavior. Addicts see themselves as victims of their circumstances and the choices of others around them. "I wouldn't drink if my spouse treated me right" or "If you hadn't gotten divorced I wouldn't have started using drugs" are classics on this list. Blaming is the addict's way of transferring responsibility for her behavior to you and others. Often, an addict will get the support of an enabler by telling a sad story to prove she has been wronged and needs help. "I asked Dad for some money to pay my rent, but he is always mad at me and refused. I don't think he loves me; otherwise he wouldn't want me to get kicked out. I can never make him happy. What do I have to do to prove myself to him?" This is a great set-up to ask an enabling mother or grandparent for money. Implied in the blaming of the father is the following:

- If you love me, you'll give me money.
- You're the nice parent. Nice parents give money.
- I'm going to see rejection as a proof you don't love me.
- If you don't give me money, you want me to be miserable and evicted.

Don't be fooled into allowing the addict to shift responsibility for her behavior to you or to others. You needn't feel the responsibility to verify her statements, although you certainly could. Your only responsibility is to set a clear boundary that you will not cross. It is best to enter into any discussion of a healthy set of boundaries with an addict by knowing in advance that you will be blamed at some point. In the long-term however, by setting these boundaries you are contributing to the addict facing her issues sooner.

- *Projection.* Even when you approach an addict in a calm, reassuring manner you run the risk of having the addict blow up and project feelings of anger, frustration, and hostility onto you or others. "Why are you trying to control me?" might be a question you are likely to hear from an addict who is trying to manipulate you into giving money or resources. "Why is that stupid idiot being so hostile?" is another example of an addict projecting her own emotional frustration onto someone else. These types of statements are confusing and are meant to position the addict in the most sympathetic light possible. The addict tries to reflect a reality in which she is not hostile, but that *you* are being hostile. *She is* not manipulative and controlling, the counselor is being controlling. On and on it goes. A good rule of thumb might be to listen for the emotions and characteristics that the addict is using to describe you and others in her life and then carefully consider if, in fact, those same issues really apply to the addict. This is a useful tool for helping to emotionally cope with the accusations and projections of the addict.

- *Minimizing.* "I only have a couple of drinks. It's not a problem" or "I'm not a drug addict. I just smoke pot" are examples of minimizing statements that addicts often make. Refusing to admit the magnitude of the problem, the addict seeks to make the issue smaller. This effectively makes it YOUR problem, not hers, so she can avoid facing the truth about her behavior. As with the other attitudes and behaviors listed here, your best tool against minimizing is to stay connected to what you know to be true and real. Unless and until the addict is ready to get real about the problem, there is no hope of solution. Addressing the reality of the problem is one of the only tools you have to help keep this issue in the forefront of the relationship. Are you really blowing this problem out of proportion? Reading this book and researching common drug-related issues will educate you about the severity of the problem. In most cases it is more likely that the problem is even bigger than you realize.

- *Guilt and threats.* Addicts will use threats of suicide, poverty and more to make the enabler feel guilty, thus enhancing the chance that they will give in to their demand. Threats of suicide should not be taken lightly, but neither should threats be used to extract enabling support. Be prepared to refer the addict to counseling if the addict verbalizes suicidal feelings.

You must be prepared to experience all of these responses when withdrawing logistical support to the addict. Even if you have a loving and caring relationship, the addict feels powerless to fight this drug and will likely view your response through the eyes of addiction, becoming frustrated, angry, and defensive, desiring to flee and wanting to lay the blame at your feet. ✚

Building Your Inner Strength

L iving with an addict is disorienting, and the magnitude of problems facing the addict—problems that enablers adopt as their own—is all-consuming. Enablers may spend their day running around town paying bills, covering the traces of wreckage the addict leaves behind. Or just as likely, enablers may become isolated, overwhelmed, embarrassed and tired. It's all they can do to get up in the morning.

Enabling takes a tremendous toll on individuals and families that get drawn into its vortex. It is critically important that you decide for yourself and your family that you are going to be healthy. Without solid determination and a plan to get more balance—as well as perspective and independence from the addict that you have become intertwined with—you will eventually run out of the emotional resources necessary to live a successful and healthy life.

Enablers often sacrifice their own future, health, family, and resources in an effort to make the life of the addict better. In some cases, the parental enabler is so focused on helping the addict that their actions breed problems in the siblings.

The other children feel neglected and become desperate for attention, having received the message that being troublesome garners attention. Thus other problems surface within the family, causing additional strain.

Jim, a heroin addict, had a pattern of creating chaos in his life. As an experienced manipulator, he would keep a mental record of which friends he had enough goodwill to ask "a favor." A phone call, a drop by the house or even bumping into an old friend would lead Jim to explain the nature of his current problem and ask for help. For enablers, this is where the handoff of emotional responsibility takes place. It's like a baton being passed to the next runner in a relay race. The only difference is that the addicts have no intention of actually handling the baton themselves. They are overwhelmed and caught up in the grips of their selfish behavior and only want the enabler to help them make their troubles go away.

A parent or spouse that is caught up in an enabling relationship feels societal pressure to handle the problems of the addict that they love. Is it society's responsibility to handle the problems of the addict or is it the family's responsibility? What is the healthy balance for a parent or spouse?

Another question arises. When we draw a firm line of responsibility with the addict—forcing him to deal with the consequences of his behavior rather than insulating him from the effects of his selfishness—how will we *maintain* the emotional strength necessary to "hold the line?" It takes personal, spiritual strength.

As you can see, there are a number of situations where an addict can force a very unhealthy and pressure filled situation onto family, friends and the community. People can become so occupied with thinking of societal consequences and worrying about their responsibilities that they forget the key ingredient: the sole responsibility for the addictive behavior and its consequences rests on the addict. The relationship must not insulate the addict from the consequences of his behavior.

To withstand the pressure of these toxic relationships you must develop patterns, habits, and support groups to help build spiritual strength for your own life.

Here are a few things to remember as you start this journey toward building a healthy life.

✚ It's not about you.

Part of the craziness of the addictive lifestyle is that in the confusion, despair, and hurt of dealing with an addict we begin to personalize the problems of the addict. Their legal problems become our concern. We feel moral outrage at the way his spouse is treating him, we cannot believe that others are not stepping forward to help solve this problem. Many other thoughts of personal outrage occur to us when we are enabling. In the end, if you are to truly face your enabling behavior and become a healthy support for your loved one who is facing addiction, you must own the fact that you have made this battle personal, and that this is wrong. Until you are able to stop personalizing the problems of the addict and making this about you—your embarrassment, your responsibility, your love, and your past mistakes—then you cannot help your loved one.

Perhaps you have made mistakes in your life that you feel may have contributed to the emotional weakness of the addict. While you can own your own mistakes, you must draw the line at assuming a direct cause and effect between *your* past decisions, and the decisions made by the addict. Enabling behavior in the present will only compound mistakes you made in the past.

A parent who has been through a messy divorce will often feel that this in some way contributed to the addiction of their child. This kind of emotional archeology is interesting and can be useful in the context of a discussion with a trained professional counselor, but when used as an emotional weapon (even if self-inflicted) to justify unhealthy support of addictive behavior, it is extremely damaging.

So it is in the marriage relationship. When a husband or wife uses their own past mistakes, inadequacies and regrets (or allows those mistakes to be used against them) as a rationale for enabling and supporting the addictive and destructive behaviors of their loved one, they are only compounding the problem.

It doesn't take a problematic marital or parental relationship for an empathic person to become so personally attached to the problems of the addict that they become an enabler. However, these burdens from the past add a complicating factor for many.

Regardless of your past mistakes, it is critically important that you understand that you cannot personalize the problems of the addict if you are to have a healthy life. The problems are NOT about you. They are connected to the chemical addiction of the alcoholic/addict, the selfish and single-minded manner in which the addict pursues fulfilling that appetite, and the resulting chaos of those efforts.

Lying and dishonest behavior doesn't necessarily mean that an addict dislikes you personally. These actions are driven by the selfishness of his addictive behavior. When the addict is not under the influence of the chemicals, he may make promises he has every intention of keeping, but finds himself unable to keep due to his crazy habit. This in no way excuses the behavior. To the contrary, he must be responsible for it. It only serves to remind you even further that it's not about you.

Often I've had mothers and fathers talk with shock about their grown child's alcohol and drug abuse with phrases such as: "My son has never lied to me. He wouldn't do that" and "We have an honest relationship, and he knows he can trust me." The key word in both of those sentences, and others like them is the word "ME." The enabler personalizes the problems, solutions, and behaviors to make them a validation or rejection of their relationship. Many times, it is clear that the enabler is acting out of selfishness. The unwillingness to deal head-on with the addict's behavior is rooted in a self-centered perspective. Not wanting to feel guilt, rejection, pressure, or add additional work to their schedule, the enabler takes the easy way out. It is not about you. It's about the addiction.

Why is it important to understand this? It is important because healthy people understand the difference between themselves and other people. This is equally true in parental and marital relationships. Healthy people are not willing to be controlled and manipulated by others through guilt trips, threats, and accusations claiming that they are responsible for actions taken by another. Neither do healthy people desire to control people by making them dependent. A healthy parental relationship goes through many stages, but hopefully results in a healthy, mutual love and respect when the child becomes an adult and the parent accepts their adult child as a peer. In addictive/enabling parental relationships, this stage is never achieved because both the parent and child (regardless of age) get stuck in the stage of provider/dependent. Frankly, there is nothing sadder than seeing an aging parent supporting an adult child in their addiction. Sometimes, as was the case with Junior in Chapter 1, the parent only realizes that their supportive behavior enables addiction when they are facing their own mortality. They won't be around to support the child and they don't know what will happen to them. By this time the adult child is unlikely to ever learn true independence.

✚ You need a plan for *your* life.

It's not uncommon for humans to concern themselves with the behavior of others, while ignoring our own short-comings, faults, and unhealthy behaviors. Recently I saw a picture book called <u>*Medical Professionals Smoking*</u>, which was a quirky way of highlighting an interesting psychological phenomenon. Why do some people who see the illness, cancer, and death of smokers more regularly than the general population still persist with smoking? Often there is a discon-nection between our perception of the behavior of others and our perception of how we behave. It is also common for us to believe that we are the exception to the rule.

Dealing with an addictive personality, you are now given a choice of whether to spend your time trying to force some-one else to be healthy, or choosing to become healthy your-self. *Make the choice to get healthy.* We cannot force anyone else to be healthy. We can only make decisions for ourselves.

The crucial first step is to get a plan for your life. Imagine what your life should look like and take steps for a healthy life, even if the addict chooses to continue in the addiction.

Over the years I've seen many parents sacrifice their

golden years, obsessed with trying to solve the addiction problem of their grown child. Only, they can't solve it for him. It's something the adult child must solve himself. Time spent obsessing over a solution, especially one that must come from a desire and commitment within the addict, only delays the possibility of a decision from the addict. Recovery is something that individuals must seek for themselves. You must begin to think about how you can build a life and future that will allow you to live your destiny, the purpose God has called *you*, in a healthy way.

✚ Healthy is *second* nature.

Looking back on my family and adolescence I can see that I have much for which to be thankful. Yet, I also know that there are false beliefs that I have brought with me into adulthood. False beliefs are those things that one has assumed to be facts, but which actually are not true. Often, addicts will carry false beliefs like, "Nobody loves me", "I can never be free from this drug", or "I'm stupid." These are false beliefs that the addict no longer questions, but believes whole-heartedly.

We all have false beliefs—things that we assume to be true—but which are in fact lies. The belief that "no one else will love me" keeps many enablers in unhealthy and abusive relationships. "If I don't help this person, no one else will" and "They'd be homeless without me," are also false beliefs.

You don't know that to be true; you just assume that in order to justify your enabling behavior. Perhaps the addict would come to recovery more quickly if you withdrew support.

Being healthy and ignoring all the patterns and false beliefs of the past is not always comfortable. We humans define as natural, those things that feel comfortable. That's why I say that being healthy is *SECOND* nature. It's something you must imagine, dream, learn and practice daily before you begin to feel comfortable.

Earlier we spoke about verbally loving and encouraging the addict. For many people this is very unnatural. Fathers are often characterized as having difficulty expressing love verbally, but it is true within all gender and cultural categories. It is not natural for many of us to let down our guard and share our emotions with words. Yet it is important and critical for healthy relationships. That's why I encourage you to do the hard work by practicing verbalizing your emotional support to the addict until it becomes second nature. In time, you can become comfortable with doing what is healthy; but not until you imagine yourself doing what is healthy and take steps to practice the healthy thing.

Don't get too frustrated if the healthy behaviors recommended in this book seem contrary to what feels natural. What feels natural is just what you are comfortable doing, not necessarily what works. This is about doing what encourages recovery.

✚ You need support

Without fail, the most common question I receive from parents and loved ones of addicts is, "What can I do?" I've tried to answer that in this small volume, but the most critical thing you can do is to become healthy yourself, both emotionally and spiritually. To do this you need support. Whether that is from within your family or church or from the support of groups such as Al-Anon and Celebrate Recovery, you need to surround yourself—overwhelm yourself—with loving and encouraging people that can understand, listen and support you in being healthy. You need support as much as the addict you are seeking to help. Without support you are likely to fall into negative, enabling patterns that will destroy you emotionally and postpone the day of recovery for the addict.

✚ A healthy future *is* possible.

A healthy future is possible so don't lose hope or feel helpless. If you are taking the steps to create a healthy environment for yourself and those you love, you are doing what you can do. Be in prayer daily for the addict you love. Addiction is not just a physical problem, but is rooted in emotional and spiritual pain. You can't solve spiritual problems with physical solutions. You must have a spiritual solution to a spiritual problem.

For many people the idea of God is abstract and it brings up negative religious experiences in their past. Yet when we face spiritual and emotional pain in our lives, I believe it is critical to examine our values and spiritual foundations.

In my life I have personally found a spiritual comfort and peace in a personal relationship with Jesus. Far from the caricature that is portrayed in religious institutions and organized religion, I have found the words and writings on the life of Jesus to be wise, loving, clear and inspirational.

Even with the overwhelming pain and emotional turmoil that addiction brings into the life of a family and individual, I find many people have had such negative religious experiences that they reject any spiritual solution and comfort. Don't make this mistake. Religions have perverted the life of Christ for their own purposes; yet the life of Jesus is rich with guidance, wisdom and comfort. Don't reject Jesus because of the failure of institutions. Don't reject spiritual solutions and spiritual strength in your life and in the life of your loved one caught in the grips of addiction to drugs and alcohol. Sobriety is an essential start, but living a life with meaning and purpose is critical to a happy life.

Encourage those in addiction to be open to God and the role of God in their life. Above all, they need a spiritual healing to bring about true peace in their life. Filled with false beliefs about their value and purpose on this earth, many addicts would literally prefer to die than live. In fact some are literally trying to commit suicide with each hit or drink they take. Can you in good conscience withhold a spiritual solution from them? Many times parents and loved ones resist encouraging addicts to get into faith-based programs for fear they will become spiritual zealots. That is a false choice. Every person, addict or not, needs to reconcile themselves with the larger questions of life: Why am I here? Is there a God? What is my purpose on this earth? What is love? What gives my life meaning? Is there forgiveness?

Seek spiritual truth and peace. Don't withhold that truth and peace from those you love who are in addiction. There is hope and a bright future for you and for those you love who are caught in addiction. ✚

NOTES

NOTES